W9-BVZ-662

A Handful of Dirt

Raymond Bial

Walker & Company   New York

Author's Note

My grandfather always seemed old to me—as old as the dirt he worked in while one season unfolded into another. Each spring repeated itself as I watched him in his garden. Divided by a brick walk, one half of my grandfather's backyard was surrendered completely to flowers. The other half was given over to vegetables and the lawn, most of which was shaded by an ancient oak tree. Back by the alley was the shed in which my grandfather kept his hoes and spades. Over the years, the handles of these tools darkened with the sweat and soil from my grandfather's hands. Next to the toolshed was the compost heap where he made more soil, so black that it absorbed the light, seemingly taking the strength of the sun into itself. My grandfather did not speak English very well, but it did not matter because he never taught with words. He lived his lessons for my mother and me—that the land has a soul. To my grandfather, the highest calling was to tend one's garden well and to make more soil.

One April day, my grandfather went into the hospital, and when I visited him I was struck by how thoroughly he did not belong in that place. I had always thought of my grandfather in the context of the sun; I had never thought of him out of the light. As I drove home that afternoon, I knew that I would never see him again. Upon his death, I received the most wondrous gifts—my grandfather's tools—spade, hoe, shovels, and rakes. I now work with these tools in my own backyard, and I still feel my grandfather's callused grip on the handles.

It came to be that I have three children—two daughters and a son—and I have taught them to enjoy the fragrance of freshly turned soil as well as the April flowers. As they have grown up, I have placed the seeds in each of their young hands. I have shown them how to enrich the earth with compost of our own making. So they too may someday teach their children not only how to bring forth abundant green but also how to make more soil. And now I give this book to you.

My grandfather's tools.

Soil is everywhere. In the country, farmers plow the soil of their sprawling fields. In the city, people spade garden patches in their backyards. The sprawling prairies grow in the soil, as do deeply rooted forests with their high canopies of branches overhead. Even the drifting sands of the deserts hold enough soil to sustain cacti and succulents. The grass and trees in yards and neighborhood parks are rooted in soil. Your house or apartment is built upon the soil, as are sidewalks and streets. Soil has settled at the bottoms of lakes, rivers, and oceans, and in the crevices of all but the highest mountain peaks. There is soil everywhere, both in far-off places and right under your feet.

Soil can be found all over the Earth: on the forest floor (top left); in the hot desert (top right); under flowing rivers (bottom right); beneath the tall prairie grass (bottom left).

Without soil there would be no life on Earth. We eat vegetables and fruit, as well as animals that feed on the grasses and grains grown in the soil. We make clothes from cotton, wool, and many other products that trace their roots back to the soil. Soil is as essential as the elements of water and air and as the energy of the sun.

Soil is made up of organic and inorganic—living and nonliving—ingredients. The inorganic minerals found in soil—clay, silt, and sand—began as rocks that have been worn down by wind and water over thousands of years. Rocks break apart when water collects in their cracks, then freezes and expands. Streams and rivers also wear down rocks, just as the ocean waves over time grind large stones into grains of sand on the beach.

Facing page: Washing back and forth, the waves of lakes and seas tumble small rocks, which are gradually broken down into tiny bits of sand.

Above: Waves persistently crashing on the shores of this lake have worn most of the stones on the beach into sand.

Silently falling from the trees, autumn leaves collect on the forest floor and gradually turn into humus.

This photograph made with an electron microscope shows the tiny bits of minerals and plant material that make up humus. The brown areas are wood fibers, the green areas are leaf parts, the purple spots are minerals, and the yellow spots are pollen.

8

Soil is also made up of organic materials that were once alive. If you pick up a handful of soil, you will be holding invisible bits of rotted leaves and grass and fragments of dead insects. The grasses and wildflowers of the prairies feed on the remains of plants that have died, just as the forest floor is covered with dead leaves that become humus—a dark, fragrant substance that feeds the trees reaching high into the sky. Earthworms, as well as bacteria and other small creatures, munch on this plant and animal matter and turn it into vital soil ingredients. Humus helps to stick crumbs of soil together, almost like glue, and enables it to hold water like a sponge.

Enriched with bits of leaves and other plant matter, this humus provides most of the nutrients needed by flowers, vegetables, and trees.

Amazingly, earthworms, like this night crawler, eat soil as they burrow through underground passages.

Microscopic clostridium bacteria break down dead plant and animal matter in the soil, releasing their nutrients to feed a new generation of growing plants.

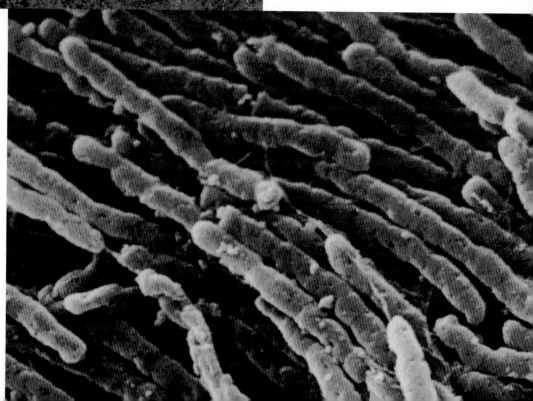

Soil may not seem to be alive, but, amazingly, most of the wild creatures of the world live in the soil. These living things range in size from microscopic bacteria that are invisible to the naked eye to wriggly earthworms up to six inches long, as well as snakes and burrowing mammals that spend at least part of their lives underground. They are more abundant and varied than the species of the tropical rain forests and the coral reefs of the South Seas combined. A single acre of land may provide food and shelter for a million ants, two hundred thousand mites, and four thousand worms.

Above: With their powerful front feet, moles tunnel through the soil, gobbling up earthworms and other underground delicacies.

Here, a fox has ambushed a bird. The bird provided a meal for the fox, and its remains will also feed plants.

As the body of this cottontail rabbit decays, nutrients will be returned to the soil to nourish prairie grasses in the next growing season.

12

Beneath the surface, millions of microscopic critters called micro-organisms battle for supremacy in their miniature world, gobbling up plant debris, animal remains, and each other! The tiniest of these living things, bacteria and protozoa, energetically devour any organic matter that touches the soil—fallen autumn leaves and roots dying underground—as well as the flesh of dead animals. Their action releases the nutrients, or food, that is then drawn up by the roots of living plants. Without these microorganisms, the soil would be unable to grow anything.

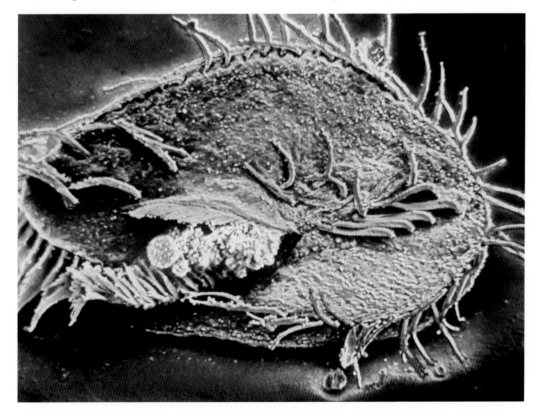

This single-celled protozoa is visible only under a microscope. It swims through the film of water that surrounds particles of soil.

Many people think of soil as unclean. Soil is popularly called "dirt," from the Old English word *drit,* meaning manure. When playing in the yard, you may get "dirty" and your clothes may become "soiled." However, through decomposition, bacteria break down diseases and other deadly substances present in dead animals so they are no longer harmful.

Fungi, including mushrooms, also decompose just about any dead organic materials, returning their nutrients to the earth. Mushrooms come in many shapes and sizes. Some are quite lovely, and others are downright ugly. Some are delicious, but many are deadly. Those with bright colors or white gills are pure poison; others, like the stinkhorn, emit foul odors. It's best to stay away from mushrooms, except those at the grocery store.

Facing page: Popping up in the woods, mushrooms are the most familiar of the fungi. They work quietly in the shade, making soils fertile for new generations of plants.

Above: Often appearing as an eerie mass, fungi devour organic matter, reducing chunks of rotting wood to humus.

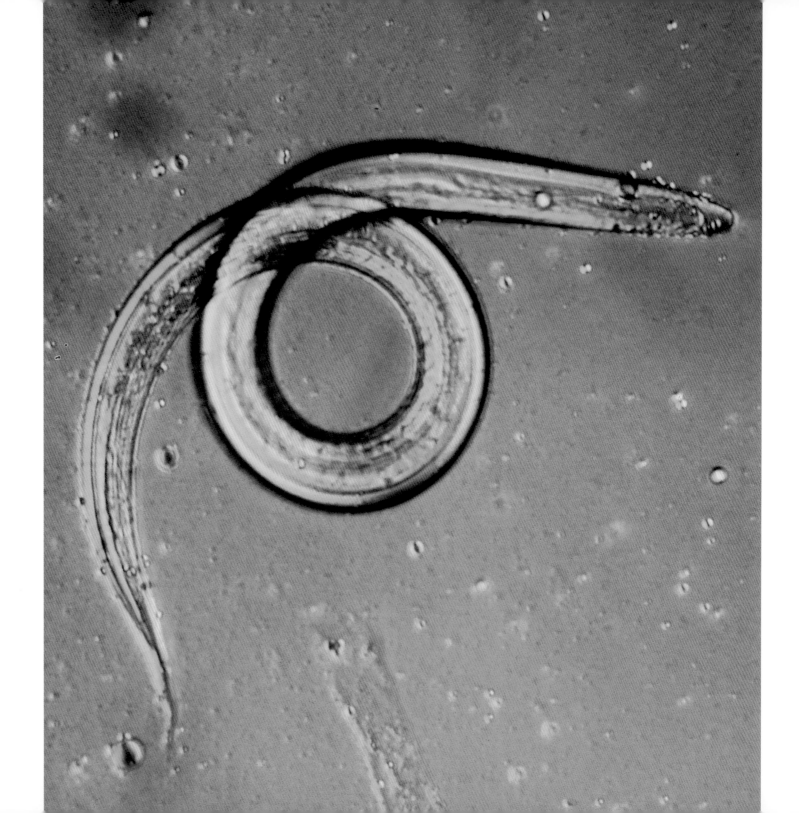

Many different kinds of worms live in the soil, including earthworms, wire worms, and nematodes. The most numerous of these squiggly organisms are the strange creatures called nematodes, which feed on bacteria. There may be a million nematodes in a single acre of land. Also called threadworms and roundworms, these eel-shaped, colorless worms are often too small to be seen except through a microscope.

Earthworms constantly burrow through the soil. Their vast networks of tunnels make excellent channels for air and water, as well as other small creatures. As many as 1,600 earthworms may live in a square meter of soil. Earthworms eat enormous amounts of leaves and other organic material—all the leaves falling to the forest floor may be devoured within a single year. With several pounds of soil passing through each of their wiggly bodies every year, they excrete waste called "castings" that further enrich the soil.

Facing page: A microscopic view of a nematode.

Above: These glistening red worms are feasting on kitchen scraps, which they will transform into compost in a matter of days.

Lubricated with slime, snails and slugs glide over plants and graze with teeth located on their undersides. Although some of these slowpokes riddle the leaves of farm crops and garden vegetables, most snails and slugs prefer to dine on dead plants.

Like tiny cattle, crickets, millipedes, sow bugs, and other tiny "grazers" nibble leaves and grasses, breaking them down into the ingredients for fertile soil. Busy ants also recycle nutrients as they tunnel and bring food underground.

Moist and sticky, a plump slug cruises over a dead leaf, one of its favorite foods (top left). Scuttling under the leaf litter, a sow bug not much larger than a grain of rice scavenges on dead plants (top right). Flatworms latch onto earthworms, viciously tear the flesh apart, and suck out the internal juices—while the worm is still alive (bottom right). Centipedes, long and flat, ably slither under rocks and fallen leaves to seize their unlucky victims. Then, with nasty pincers, they shoot a dose of deadly poison (bottom left).

Like a science fiction thriller, the surface of the soil is the battleground for the most vicious, bloodthirsty creatures on Earth. Roaming the leaf litter and mulch, as well as the leaves and stems of green plants, these ruthless, efficient predators capture and kill their prey in their razor-sharp jaws and pincers. This rogues' gallery includes praying mantises, ladybugs, and centipedes, all of which feed on the small creatures that make soil. These backyard assassins are everywhere, but their slaughter is hardly noticed in their small "eat or be eaten" world, except that many useful plants are spared from the ravenous appetites of the crickets and aphids upon which they prey.

Facing page: With their gruesome-looking jaws, sticklike praying mantises resemble alien creatures from outer space as they munch on backyard insects.

Ladybugs appear to be dainty and kind, but these useful predators devour huge numbers of aphids, tiny insects that suck the living juices from plants.

This garter snake feeds primarily on insects and worms living in or near the soil.

As they graze on a slope on the northern plains, these cattle not only feed on grass but also help to fertilize the soil with their manure.

These insects in turn are gobbled up by the reptiles, including snakes and lizards, and mammals, such as moles, gophers, and prairie dogs, that make their homes in the earth. Moles plow along, just beneath the surface, gobbling up worms, grubs, and roots—they rarely appear above ground in the light of day. Ground squirrels, gophers, and prairie dogs tunnel deep into the ground, churning up tons of subsoil, especially in sandy and gravelly land, because they prefer dry places. These burrowing animals mix plant material and their droppings into the soil.

Larger, grazing animals, such as cattle and sheep, fertilize the soil with manure, which is chockful of nutrients. They also nibble grasses, leaving bite-sized bits on the ground to be whittled down further by insects and microorganisms.

Facing page: Digging vast networks of tunnels, prairie dogs haul bits of plants to their underground nests and thoroughly mix up the soil.

A garden or a field is only as good as its soil. The best soil allows air, water, and nutrients to reach the roots easily. One of the best ways to enrich soil is to apply home-grown compost—plants just love the dark, crumbly humus. Compost is made naturally in forests and grasslands from dead leaves, roots, and stems, but you can make your own compost in your backyard.

To decay properly, the compost pile needs the right amounts of carbon and nitrogen. Carbon-rich materials, such as leaves raked in the autumn, are known as "browns." Nitrogen-rich materials, such as fresh grass clippings, vegetable and fruit scraps from your kitchen, and weeds pulled from the garden, are called "greens." Compost piles with a mixture of browns and greens in a ratio of about twenty-five to one decompose quickly and yield the richest compost.

Facing page: Gardeners know the value of compost, which they apply in large amounts to their beds of flowers and vegetables.

Mixed together in the right amounts, greens and browns quickly decompose to make excellent compost.

To make your own compost, find a shady spot in the yard and alternate layers of fallen leaves (browns) and grass clippings or weeds (greens), along with a little soil or fresh compost, in a pile at least three feet high and wide. The soil or compost will supply hungry microorganisms that will get right to work on the fresh organic materials. Spray the pile with a garden hose, until it is sponge damp, and make sure it stays moist but not soggy. To keep everything mixed up, you can turn the pile with a garden fork every week or so. Or you can simply leave the heap alone. The compost is finished when most of the mixture is dark and crumbly. The process may take from a month to a year or more, depending on whether you turn the pile or not, but you'll end up with a mound of rich, fragrant compost.

Facing page: These three bins show the stages of composting right to left—dead plants, partially decomposed matter, and finished compost.

Right: Compost heaps must be occasionally watered to help the leaves and grass clippings rot away.

The cycle of life, death, and decay in the soil continues to this very moment. Every second of every day soil is being made, just as it was millions of years ago. And if you make more soil, you'll be helping to create a better world for all of us. However, every second of every day soil is also being lost—to wind, water, and the growth of cities where the soil is buried under asphalt or cement. The next time you play in your backyard or the neighborhood park, think of the soil beneath your feet. It may not seem to be worth very much, but remember, soil is as precious as the wind in your face and the sun warming your shoulders.

Facing page: These children are working peat moss into the soil and having a little fun as they prepare their backyard garden for spring planting.

Further Reading

Many excellent books about soil—and making more soil through composting—have been published. Here are some of the books that were consulted in writing A Handful of Dirt:

Ball, Liz. *Composting*. New York: Workman Publishing, 1998.

Biondo, Ronald J. *Introduction to Plant and Soil Science and Technology*. Danville, Ill.: Interstate Publishers, 1997.

Brady, Nyle C. *The Nature and Properties of Soils*. Upper Saddle River, N.J.: Prentice Hall, 1996.

Butler, Orton C. *An Introductory Soils Laboratory Handbook*. Hicksville, N.Y.: Exposition Press, 1979.

Campbell, Sue. *Let It Rot! The Gardener's Guide to Composting*. Pownal, Vt.: Storey Publishing, 1998.

Epstein, Eliot. *The Science of Composting*. Lancaster, Penn.: Technomic Pub. Co., 1997.

Harpstead, Milo I.; Thomas J. Sauer; and William F. Bennett. *Soil Science Simplified*. Ames, Iowa: Iowa State University Press, 1997.

Hattey, Jeffory A. *Fundamentals of Soil Science: A Laboratory Manual*. Dubuque, Iowa: Kendall/Hunt Pub. Co., 1996.

Logan, William Bryant. *Dirt: The Ecstatic Skin of the Earth*. New York: Riverhead Books, 1995.

Miller, Raymond W. *Soils in Our Environment*. Upper Saddle River, N.J.: Prentice Hall, 1998.

Minnich, Jerry, et al. *The Rodale Book of Composting*. Emmaus, Penn.: Rodale Press, 1992.

Nancarrow, Loren. *The Worm Book: The Complete Guide to Growing Earthworms for Composting and Gardening*. Berkeley, Calif.: Ten Speed Press, 1998.

Ondra, Nancy J. *Soil and Composting: The Complete Guide to Building Healthy, Fertile Soil*. Boston: Houghton Mifflin, 1998.

Palmer, Robert G. *Introductory Soil Science: Laboratory Manual*. New York: Oxford University Press, 1995.

Singer, Michael J. *Soils: An Introduction*. Upper Saddle River, N.J.: Prentice Hall, 1996.

Stell, Elizabeth. *Secrets to Great Soil: A Grower's Guide to Composting, Mulching, and Creating Healthy, Fertile Soil for Your Garden and Lawn*. Pownal, Vt.: Storey Publishing, 1998.

Troeh, Frederick R. and Louis M. Thompson. *Soils and Soil Fertility*. New York: Oxford University Press, 1993.

Webber, Eldon C. *Earthworm Empire: The Living Soil*. Dubuque, Iowa: Kendall-Hunt Publishing Co., 1996.

White, R. E. *Principles and Practice of Soil Science: The Soil as a Natural Resource*. Oxford; Malden, Mass.: Blackwell Science, 1997.

There are a number of fine books for children about soil, which were also helpful in writing this book:

Dewey, Jennifer Owings. *Mud Matters*. New York: Marshall Cavendish, 1998.

Keen, Martin L. *The World Beneath Our Feet: The Story of Soil*. New York: Julian Messner, 1974.

Simon, Seymour. *Beneath Your Feet*. New York: Walker and Co., 1977.

Index

Page numbers in italics refer to photo captions

This book is dedicated to my mother, Catherine Bial, and my grandfather, Joe Jackse, who taught me to appreciate the soil.

First published in the United States of America in 2000 by Walker Publishing Company, Inc.

Photograph credits: page 8 © Dennis Kunkel; page 10 © David M. Phillips/Visuals Unlimited; page 11 © John Sohlden/Visuals Unlimited; page 13 © K.G. Murti/Visuals Unlimited; page 16 © Arthur M. Siegelman/Visuals Unlimited; page 20 © P. Lindholm/Visuals Unlimited; page 21 © Tom Edwards/Visuals Unlimited; pages 31 and 32 Ed Zaborski; all other photos copyright Raymond Bial.

I would like to express my deepest appreciation to my children, Sarah and Luke, who appear in the book, and to my wife, Linda, for her help in making the photographs.

I would also like to thank Ed Zaborski of the Illinois Natural History Survey for his kind assistance with this project.

Library of Congress Cataloging-in-Publication Data

Bial, Raymond.
    A handful of dirt/Raymond Bial.
        p.   cm
    Includes bibliographical references.
    Summary: Discusses the nature and importance of soil and the many forms of life it supports.
    ISBN 0-8027-8698-7 (hardcover)—ISBN 0-8027-8699-5 (reinforced)
    1. Soils—Juvenile literature. 2. Soil ecology—Juvenile literature. [1.Soils 2. Soil ecology. 3. Ecology.] I. Title
S591.3.B53 2000
577.5'7'0222—dc21

                                    99-053632

Book design by Diane Hobbing/SNAP-HAUS GRAPHICS

Printed in China by South China Printing Company, Dongguan, Guangdong

10 9 8